Spinalonga,
the Island of the "living dead"

Antonis Alibertis

Spinalonga,
the Island of the "living dead"

MYSTIS©
EDITIONS

Iraklio, 2011

Text –photography: **Antonis Alibertis**
12 Atalandis St, 71409, Heraklion, Crete, Greece
tel: +302810323398
e-mail: alibertant@gmail.com

Editorship: **Nikos Dretakis**

Translation: **Zoe Antonopoulou**
e-mail: antozoe@gmail.com

Print-out/Bookbinding:
TYPOKRETA
VI.PE. Heraklion
tel: +302810380882
e-mail: typokreta@her.forthnet.gr
webpage: www.kazanakis.gr

MΥΣΤΙΣ©
E D I T I O N S

Antonis Tsintaris & Co
108 Menelaou Parlama St., 71500, Iraklio, Crete, Greece
tel: +302810346451
fax: +302810221908
e-mail: info@mystis.gr
webpage: www.mystis.grI

ISBN: 978-960-6655-80-7

CONTENTS

Spinalonga was the name given by the Venetians to the peninsula Kolokitha as well as the small island, which today goes by the same name, a complex, which today is thought that at those times was connected by land. This complex, consisting of two small islands, looks more like a spinal cord and less than a long sting, as the Italian expression "spina longa" conveys.

Indeed, looking at Kolokitha and Spinalonga islands from Elouda bay, early in the morning, before sunrise, it's obvious that what Venetians meant by this expression is the grand spinal cord which forms before the observer' s eyes. Hence, the name apparently emerges from the expression "spina dorsale longa", meaning "grand spinal cord". There are others who suggest that the name Spinalonga comes from the Venetian paraphrase of the Greek words "στην Ελούντα"-"Stinelouda" (meaning "at Elouda bay"), a phrase that as time went by turned into "Stinalonde" then "Stinalonde", then "Istinalonga" and finally Spinalonga, though this version is considered rather extreme.

A First Image

Traveling from Agios Nikolaos and arriving for the first time at the neck leading to Elouda bay and Plaka, you might be swept by the pastoral scene unraveling before the eyes.

This place looks magical, has a sense of tranquility and serenity. The greatness of the moment is breathtaking.

Low, just above sea level, the luxurious tourist blocks compete in beauty. A little further away there is Poros, a narrow strip of land connecting the islands, with its impressive, ancient windmills. On its left hand side there is the abandoned Venetian salt works, reminding of a marshland and on its right there is Kolokitha island, stretching leisurely, parallel to the land, with its mountain-line oriented north-to-south into the deep blue of the Merambellos gulf. Right here, at Poros, the ancient city of Olous or Olouda is sunk deep into the sea, into the kingdom of Poseidon, probably because of a sudden collapse of the earth. A bit further away, somewhere between Kolokitha island and the land of Crete, the wind-protected, small gulf of Korfos appears, a natural port, perfectly protected by bad weather and the eyes of the enemy, bearing on its deepest end the today's white city of Elouda.

At the entrance of Korfos, located on a valuable for the control of the port spot, at the very north end of Kolokitha island, across the scenic fishermen's village Plaka, there is a small island, surrounded by walls, looking artificial.

This is the legendary island of Spinalonga, as it was called by the Venetians, Spirlonga of the Turks, the island of the "living dead". (page14-15)

Left hand side, up. A current road-sign, located at the neck, depicting the area of interest.

Left hand side, down. Spinalonga port. Photograph borrowed from the Olfert Dapper map (1688).

Right hand side. Poros.

The History of the Island

FROM THE ANCIENT TIMES
TO THE ARRIVAL OF THE VENETIANS

*S*pinalonga looks like a mountain at sea, like a limestone bed of rocks that covers an area of no more than eighty five square kilometers. On the island there hasn't been found any traces of the Minoan civilization. However, during the Ancient Times and specifically the Hellenic period, when Olous or Olounda was at its peak, sustaining a Sanctuary, an organized port and its own currency, it is thought that the first works of fortification took place at the north-west part of the island and along its ridge. These are today known by the writings of the Venetian engineers, who supervised the fortification works and also by the original blue-print model, which is a safe-guarded exhibit at the Museo Storico Navale at Venice. Of those early fortification works, only a few parts were used during the latter, imposing work on the fortress. The rest were probably destroyed or build over, during the earthing of the ground for the founding of the latter fortress.

Since the period from the abandonment of the ancient city of Olounda, when Crete was taken over by the Arabs Saraceans of Abu Hafs Umar Aysi, the Andalusian (827-961), also known as Apochapsis and the regaining of the land by Nikiforos Fokas (961-1204), when the island was under the Venetian occupation, there is barely any information about the island and the area around it. The only documents left today are a few worn out by time murals on the walls of the now deserted church of Agios Nikolaos, which can tell the story of the first Byzantine period.

Page on the right
1. The salt works, as they appear today.
2. The salt works of Elouda, 1948.
3. The salt works of Elouda, 1960: Workers piling salt.
(Photos 2 and 3 are taken from the book "Elouda" by M. Makrakis)

16

VENETIAN PERIOD (1204-1715)

*D*uring the Kingdom of Chandax (Regno di Candia) in Crete, but mostly during 15th century, the Venetians built salt works, which today are still preserved in good shape on the shallow and rich in salt waters of the gulf, southern of today's Elouda bay. The largest part of the production of salt was shipped to Venice and Europe. Those times were

relatively quiet up until the beginning of the 16th century, when the looting of the largest part of eastern coastal Crete by the famous pirate Hayreddin Barbarossa, also known as Redbeard, during 1537-1538, his physical presence for a long time at the port of Korfos, as well as the Turkish threat, which became even greater after the occupation of Cyprus at 1570, made the Venetians suspicious. The Venetians, bearing in mind that the eastern sea frontiers of their domain had to retreat to Crete, they decided to fortify the island the best they could, in an effort to push back the forthcoming Turkish threat and sustain communication with Asia and connection to the markets of India. The whole island of Crete and specifically Spinalonga island suddenly obtained the highest strategic significance.

In 1571 the Venetian senate decided on the fortification of Spinalonga island. In 1578, the project was assigned to the experienced engineer Genese Bressani and the works started a year later, in accordance to the guidelines of the fortification system of those times, which demanded rectilinear walls and projecting bastions, so the defenders would be able to fight the enemy from the rear. The first founding stone was placed on the 15th June 1579, a work which was supervised by the general intendant fort Crete, Luca Michiel. The works proceeded fast and the lowest and most difficult to built part of the fortification, which surrounds the island at sea level, was almost over, when the initial plans changed. In 1584, the military commandant of Crete, Latino Orsini, when visiting Spinalonga island, realized that those founding fortification works at sea level could be easily struck by the enemy from the surrounding hills of Kolokitha and Vroucha. In order to combat such an attack by the enemy's artillery system, he demanded a second line of fortification and defense to be built on top of the island. Therefore, two new sections were designed, crosswise,

parallel to the first wall, the first located north-east, the second north-west, in order to connect the two main fortifying fronts. For the completion of the works, the materials used were already-carved stones taken from the ancient city of Olouda, limestone rocks from the pit next to Agios Panteleimonas at the centre of the village of Spinalonga and soft bluestone, or "ammouda", as the locals like to call it, which is found in abundance on the eastern side of Spinalonga and the nearby Kolokitha island. Those fortifying works were named after the Venetian notables, who designed the blueprints and supervised the works. Hundreds of people with a variety of skill – stonecutters, architects, technicians, builders and carpenters – people living in the nearby villages, as well as people living at different parts of Crete, like Sitia, Ierapetra, Chania, Chandax (Heraklion) and Rethimnon,

worked on a daily basis for the completion of this grand work. The Venetian Navy, the famous galleys, was also present, helping with the transportation of the appropriate soil for earthing and stones for the completion of the wall works.

In her book "Island Within Walls", Maria Arkadaki comments on the completion of the fortress:

"The story, found in references, about on the completion of the fortress, is dark and depressive, drowned in sweat, blood and pain. Hundreds of workers from nearby villages, craftsmen, galley rowers, soldiers and officers from Venice lived here for months and years, undergoing incredible pain and deprivation, with no water, rare at those times, that had to be transported from Kalo Chorio river, with insufficient food, with no roof under their heads other than temporary wooden shacks, with no communication to the outside world. The current state of the walls, specially at those steep edges of the island, indicates that the construction must have caused many human lives, owing to scaffolding accidents due to strong winds, let alone the hardship and the diseases due to unclean water".

So this small island was transformed into one of the most important sea fortresses of the Mediterranean Sea and still is, even today, a bright example of the genius of those bright Venetian engineers and those local craftsmen. The quality of the construction is exceptional, since time does not seem to have any deterioration effect.

During 17th century and in particular after the invasion of Crete by the Ottomans in 1645, additional fortification work took place, like construction of open-air cannon fenestras and elevation of the walls, though these works were poorly attended to, because of the difficult circumstances in times of war and also because of limited financial support.

During the Venetian period, the fortress was under the command of one intendant, one higher official and a few lower in rank officers. The guard was comprised of 200 to 300 men. Public houses were built, military quarters, a hospital, powder store rooms, food and military equipment store rooms, bakeries, windmills for grinding the grain, churches and big rain-water tanks. Initially, the fortress was armed with thirty five cannons and the personal amour of each soldier. Then, in 1699, when guns were transported from Chania, the armament was significantly supported.

During 1657, when most parts of Crete were under Turkish occupation, Spinalonga opened its gates to Christian

fugitives and rebels (Chainides), as well as to all those who were employed on the fortifying works. At that time, the number of the occupants of the island went up to 470 people and the city was divided into seven districts, each of which had its own church. Today, only three of those churches are saved: The church of Agios Nikolaos (page 16-69), Agios Georgios and Agios Panteleimon.

Spinalonga was surrendered to the Turks in 1715, after a knock-out blockade, which lasted three whole months, when at the same time Souda, the other fortified island of Crete, was already taken. Unfortunately, during surrender, things went wrong. Zuan Francesco Justiniani, the intendant of Spinalonga, gave the island to Kapoudan Pasa, though the conditions of the agreement were not followed by the Turks, as promised. The Venetians managed to arrive to Venice, though most of the locals were imprisoned and sold as slaves.

During this sixty five year period, up until Spinalonga was surrendered to the Turks, the island was a perfect hideaway for Chainides, the Cretan rebels, who no longer bearing the massacres, the killing, the hanging, the looting, the slavery, that was implemented from day one to the island, decided to leave the cities and found refuge in the mountains, starting guerilla-war, rebelling non-stop, up until 1898, when the last of the Turks left Crete.

Page on the left, Souda fortress.

THE ERA OF THE TURKISH OCCUPATION (1715-1903)

After surrender, 200 to 300 men were settled on the island, under the command of a Turkish higher official, who in turn reported to the pasha of Chandax (Heraklion). Sometime later, a few more Muslim families moved to Spinalonga for security reasons.

The port was abandoned and as the time went by, the people living on the island were so isolated, inside the walls, that they even lost touch with the nearby Christian population of Merambellos. Even those European travelers, who visited Crete at those times, never managed to see Spinalonga with their own eyes.

Everything changed in the middle of the 19th century, initially with the anew activation of the port and later with the arrival of many Muslims, who could no longer stand the violence between Christian and Muslim population of Crete and asked, for their security and protection, to be transferred behind the so powerful walls of the island. Indeed, during 1956, Veli Pasha issued permission to the port of Spinalonga for export trade and the people who lived on the island seized the chance. The trade was strong, as well as the trafficking, more sailors

23

appeared, more jobs created and the population of the island grew stronger, so in 1879 Spinalonga was declared a separate borough, counting 1,112 inhabitants.

In that way, Spinalonga turned out to be the largest Muslim centre of the area, an Ottoman school was built, offering basic, 4th grade education and high school education, while many trading companies moved the

period, when the Turks lived together with the Greeks on the island, many things changed. Most of the interior Venetian buildings were destroyed or deteriorated, though the main streets were not only sustained, but also renovated with additional work. At the same period, the inhabitants of Spinalonga paved a network of alleys, most of them leading to the top of the hill, since new houses

Spinalonga island during 1901 (photography: Giuzzeppe Gerrolla).

head offices on the island. The financial development, the shipping and the trade brought Muslims and Christians of the area closer together and as a consequence their transactions grew strong. It is worth noting that at the time there were twenty seven merchant shops in the market of Spinalonga. Of course, during this 188 years

were constructed further away from the sea. The Muslim cemetery was situated on the eastern side of the island, low by sea level, parallel to the interior wall and next to Scaramella bastion and Agios Georgios church. The catholic church of Agia Varvara –today's hospital- was turned into a mosque.

The main entrance was left untouched, while the market was expanded to the southern part of the main street, leading all the way out of the tunnel and the walls. The settlement was divided into eight boroughs, each answering to Turkish and Greek names, such as Bei Sternisi, Mousouloukia (fountains), Khoum Kapi (Sand Door), Lower Mosque, Kemer Alti (Underneath the Door),

Taken from the book "Elouda" by Manolis Makrakis.

Disdar, Sultan Ahmet and Tsarsi Limani or Waterfront. The Venetian-built water tanks were no longer sufficient and two new, big, communal basins were constructed, one inside the village, at Tiepolo bastion, the other in front of Agios Georgios church, facing the sea, on the eastern part of the island. According to statistic reports of the time, the water tanks on the island were, at that time, eleven in total.

During the rebellion of 1897 and after the obscure political agenda arising in Crete, Spinalonga went through financial decline. The island was besieged and bombarded by the artillery of the rebels following the commands of Aristotelis Korakas, who had settled on the hills of Vrouchas and the island may have fallen, if a French war ship hadn't arrived in time. The great forces of that era –England, France, Russia and Italy- had divided Crete into influence zones. So while Lasithi was under the protection of France, a French squad counting one hundred men, answering to lieutenant Dupourque, disembarked to Spinalonga and the Turkish guard –around 200 soldiers- was forced to walk out. With them, most of the Turkish inhabitants left and found refuge on the coast of Asia Minor.

The declaration of the Cretan State in 1898 and the 30th May 1903 decision to expel all the lepers who were living in Crete, in areas outside the cities' walls, in neighborhoods called Meskinies, and move them to Spinalonga island, forced the last Turkish inhabitants to abandon Spinalonga.

THE TIMES OF THE OPERATION OF THE LEPER SANATORIUM (1904-1957)

The first lepers moved in Spinalonga during 1904 and continued to arrive on the island in waves, leaving Crete. However, since 1913 and onwards, when Crete was united to Greece, lepers arrived on the island, coming not only from other parts of Greece, but also from other countries, too. In the beginning, the medical treatment offered was rudimentary, since the only carers were some women, working there to help the severely ill. Later, the government of Eleftherios Venizelos tried to improve the quality of life and treatment of the lepers, though the international community was not sufficiently equipped with the means of facing this terrible and really old illness.

Up until 1930, a thousand men and women were isolated in Spinalonga island, marooned, away from their families, each day facing the illness and the survival needs, on this water-barren and rocky island.

Decrees and laws defined their daily way of living, such as:

- The entrance to the island was forbidden to all, except those working at the leper sanatorium and the family members of those ill, who nonetheless had to get permission.
- The clothes had to be cleaned, exclusively on the island.
- All the items coming out of the leper sanatorium, such as letters or money, had to be properly disinfected.
- Fishing was not permitted in a distance less than two hundred meters from the island.
- The yellow flag –a symbol of infectious disease- had to be up, every day on the island.
- The dead had to be buried on the island.
- The regular staff, in charge of administration, guarding and cleaning the island, comprised of the doctor, the caretaker, three road sweepers and the priest.
- The director-doctor cared for the lepers for free, updated the records of the leper sanatorium and published his scientific observations on a yearly basis.
- The two grocery shops, that were licensed to work on the island, had to sell products in prices, set by the prefecture.
- Finally, a poor allowance of fifty five drachmas was given to each patient.

The living circumstances were difficult, especially to those who were on the terminal stages of the illness. There were people with no legs, or with one leg, others with no arms or one arm, people who had lost their vision and others, so disfigured, that no one could lay eyes on them. However, those people lived together, in those same houses abandoned by the Turks, confined, as in a prison, within this reportedly gallant fortress. Of those who reached the island every so often, some decided to end their lives, jumping from the walls to the sea rocks and into the sea, while others tried to escape by swimming away, though most tried to live a life as humane as possible and never lost hope that one day they would be cured and lived again as common people.

On the "community of the lepers" there was definitely a kind of social life. Everyone worked, even with one arm or one leg, there was significant help offered, they would

The boat of the leper sanatorium sails to Spinalonga (taken from the book "Elouda", by Manolis Makrakis).

dig their gardens (the island is divided into small parts of land, marked by stone walls), fish, work in their shops, have fun, go to the cinema –that was built during the final stages of the leper sanatorium- hear the news from fishermen and locals who worked on the island, fall in love, get married and have healthy children, who, after medical examination, were given away to relatives or orphanages. From 1938 and onwards, those children were sent to Agia Varvara Hospital of Contagious Illnesses in Athens, where they were medically examined and cared for, up until they reached adulthood.

The oldest non-Greek script mentioning the leper sanatorium dates back to 1928. The article's title is "Spinalonga, the Island of the Lepers", published by the French magazine *Illustration*, written by the French director of the Pasteur Institute in Tunis, Charles Nicole, who visited Spinalonga in 1927. This article is a record of the testimonies of the patients, living on the island at those times:

"Their sole fun and enjoyment, when not working, is looking at the sea and playing a few games and musical instruments. However, most of the time they damn their luck, drink alcohol, get drunk, fight with each other, love each other... And what if out of negligence there is someone, among those confined people, who is healthy? ... And also, of those who are not so ill...how many do they consider themselves undeservedly restricted on this island?... Many decided to fell in the sea and died, aiming to escape this terrible prison, while others managed to escape swimming...".

During 1930s, the situation in the colony took a noticeable turn for the better. New buildings were constructed, like the two priories on the northwest side of the island and an expansion of the hospital took place. Those works were financially supported by donations of socially eminent people of the times, like Koukouvas and Kalokairinos, as well as the arrival of educated people, bringing innovating ideas with them. More than that, the dynamics of the community changed significantly, when a large number of those people, under the guidance of the newly-arrived and very active student of Law School in Sitia, Epaminodas Remoundakis, founded the "Fellowship of the Ill of Spinalonga Island". Those, among others, took the initiative and brought "whitewash for the decontamination of the houses, to take away the bad smell that was tearing the nostrils and planted trees".

Staff, working at Spinalonga. Third from the right is Ep. Remoundakis (taken from the book "Elounda", by Manolis Makrakis).

Northwest side, the two priories..

28

They obtained electric generator and there was finally electrical power on the island, at times when people living in Plaka and the nearby coastal villages of Crete were using oil lamps. They organized cleaning services for the needs of the common spaces. Thanks to those people, the island acquired a theatre, a cinema, coffee shops and barber's shops, while loudspeakers were placed on the streets, sounding classical music. People started to practice different professions, a rudimentary trade was under development, there was a school with a leper teacher and finally the started publishing a small satirical magazine. However, the most important achievement of doctor Remoundakis was the uplift in the spirit, the sense of solidarity and communal help, which made quality of life reminding the good quality of their life in the past, before the illness.

Unfortunately, preposterous destruction has been reported at those times, when the inhabitants blew up parts of the Venetian wall, using dynamite, in their effort to open up the north-eastern road, which would allow a walk around the island.

During that period, "the staff comprised of an administrative director, an accountant, five nurses, a disinfector, a priest, eight boatmen, ten women who washed the clothes and ten women who offered care to the lepers". According to Manolis Foundoulakis, a leper under treatment on the island, "from a moment on, this island was no longer hell. It was a village of prisoners, with its good, bad, ill-mannered and rebel people".

(Upper picture)
Inscription on a cement pavement on the eastern side of the island.

(Left picture)
Manolis Foundoulakis

(Lower picture)
The expanded hospital

It is also said that during the war, the Germans and the Italians, while fortifying the Cretan shores, opposite Spinalonga, being afraid of an attack by the Allies, did not dare stepping foot in Spinalonga. This allowed the broadcast of underground radio shows; indeed, the doctor-director Grammatikakis copied the London and Cairo news and distributed leaflets to the inhabitants.

During the final phase of the leper sanatorium, the nearby village of Plaka showed marked development. Many of the administrative and medical staff –since they wanted to live close to their workplace- rented houses at Plaka, the village opposite to Spinalonga, in Crete. Plaka was also a stopping point for those relatives wishing to visit the ill.

In the meantime, the advancements in medicine were drastic. In 1948, a new therapy for leprosy was discovered and its application was found favourable to those with the disease. Social rehabilitation was now possible and in 1957 the leper sanatorium closed its gates for good.

There was a period (1957-1970) of abandonment and looting from locals and others, making the island looking more leper than its former inhabitants.

Today, the island is under the sponsorship of the 13th Conservancy of Byzantine Antiquities.

Upper picture, Spinalonga during abandonment.
Picture on the left, the staff of the leper sanatorium
(photos borrowed from the Spinalonga museum)

Short expedition

BY BOAT FROM PLAKA

E ven though Plaka looks quite different today since the times of the leper sanatorium, it still is a small village with fish-taverns and beautiful, short houses, regardless of the fact that the tourist complexes are only a breath away.

The sea wall, as it is today. On its end, a fisherman is working on his nets. The image seems to have risen untouched from the depths of Centuries, an illusion of time –he might as well be an ancient fisherman from Olouda, a Byzantine, a Venetian or Turk, a local Cretan, even a leper.

Image from the filming of the Greek TV series "The Island".
The characters Giorgis, Eleni and young Dimitris are
on the way to Spinalonga.

The boatman is waiting! "Walking with great difficulty to reach the dock, she leaned to her father's shoulders… The boatman untied the rope –there was nothing more to be said or to be done- and their journey begun… It was the break of a journey with no return, heading to the onset of a new life, a life in a colony of lepers, the life of Spinalonga"*

Of course, this is not the same boat. This one is new, big and fast, transporting tourists and visitors to the island. We are embarking… "Full speed ahead to the island!"…

---

*Abstract from the book "The Island" by Victoria Hislop.

In a few minutes we are about to arrive to the rocky pier... And we are here!... The greatness of the island, its imposingness... The Venetian castle is overwhelming!

According to Hislop's novel, the boats that carried the lepers arrived here and in this same spot, the director of the island was welcoming them, walked them to the colony, strolling though this old Venetian tunnel, hidden inside the socket of the extraordinary Tiepolo bastion, familiarising them with their new home.

Actually, the lepers reached the island through the old Venetian port and walked through the grand Porta Maestra stone entrance. At those times, the ill might not realise its beauty, as we perceive it today. They saw the iron bars and may thought of the inscription Dante saw at the entrance of Hell:

"I walk towards the grieved land
I [walk] towards the undying pain
I [walk] towards the damned souls
....
Leave all hope, as you walk through"

TRAVELING BY BOAT

The boat takes a turn on the last cape of Kolokitha island and Spinalonga appears before the eyes like a stone, armoured war boat, shipped there for centuries, at the entrance of the small gulf. The fortification works are still strong and gallant. The Venetians were masters in fortification constructions. The walls are located at sea level, as well as on the top of the hill. The observer can stroll their eyes, welcoming the mass of images and information, which seems to appear in a slow, cinematographic motion.

On the left hand side, the square Donato bastion is looking over the narrow strip of sea of 100 meters, between Spinalonga and Kolokitha islands.

At sea level, Bondumiero or Scaramella bastion is forming an obtuse angle, with a rectilinear and auricular (curvilinear) front (orecchione), its cannon fenestras are open-air and on its end there is a circular, closed, dome-like watch tower. Just behind it there is Agios Georgios, a two-sanctum church. The reason this church has two sanctums –built under the supervision of general intendant of Crete Loukas Michael- in August, 1599, is because Christians of both cults, orthodox and catholic, would be able to worship. From the top of the steep hill you can see the Miani artillery square and the Veniera wall, directed to the sea.

Then, there is a rather long wall with a small gate, ending to the Rangone peak, probably leading nowhere. The small, well-preserved watch tower stands out, just above

the waves. Here, during recent reconstruction works, an inscription was found, quoting the name of the special intendant Geronimo Marini, who in 1651 worked on and reconstructed the walls during the war of Crete:

"Durante turcarum bello, vir nobilis et egregious Hieronymus Marinus Provisor extraordinarius mandavit tutelam fortitudinis moenia cons: Erve que, adimplevit anno ab Incarnatione Domini... MDCLI". On the top of the hill you can clearly see the Orsini pre-bastion, accompanied by Grimani wall.

The main wall continues above the waves up to the small, wooden bridge, which is now lost and from Contarini point, a breath-taking door gives way to a downwards and dangerous path, leading to the battlements of the firs wall.

On this same spot, the wall on the top of the hill converges, is renamed Traversa Molina wall, climbs sideways following the path, becomes bulgy and dangerous and – as its name denotes- integrates with the walls at the edge of the island.

At the sharp edge of the north side of the island, a gallant bastion, just above the sea, the half-moon [mezzaluna] Michiel bastion, blocks the way. On its outer surface, an inscription with big, carved letters denotes the name of the constructor and the year of the beginnings of the construction work.

"LUCAS MICHAEL, PROVVEDITOR GENERALIS CRETAE, IL ANNO MDLXXIX": Lucas Michael, general indendant of Crete, year 1579.

On the right and left hand side of the bastion there are steep rocks with a complementary wall on top. Higher above, on the Perina steep slope, you may see Mosta and Moreta supportive fortified locations, which controlled the 800 meters wide strip of sea between Spinalonga and the shores of Crete. It was truly difficult for enemy ships to come closer, since they would be attacked by cannons!

Beyond ness, on the north-western side of the island, the long wall of the north frontier stretches, embodying parts of the ancient fortification.

43

Then, you may spot Perino angle (fianco), with its characteristic circular watch-tower, situated at the far end and in front of the two leper priories, a work which was completed during 1937, following a generous donation of 15,000 British pounds, offered by Michalinos of Chios and Kalokerinos of Heraklion.

Genese angle
(upper photograph on the right hand side)

This older photograph depicts the old Venetian port and the main gate to the castle. Looking at the port, on the right hand side, you may see the old oven, which was used for the decontamination of the items leaving Spinalonga.

Here, you may see the bridge (ponte) and the Bembo point and behind them the church of Agios Panteleimon, guardian of the ill, the vesidential houses and the public buildings. The Venetians built their small town on the north-western side of the island, since they knew that this spot would offer protection from strong winds and invaders, such as Genovese, Turks, Maltese and Algerians. Of course there were additional reasons for fortifying this island. Their trade was one of the most profitable of the ones in Europe. They imported goods from India, Africa and Middle East, like fabrics, carpets, silk, wheat, spices, pearls, precious stones etc. The Venetian empire was in need of intermediate ports, like the port of Spinalonga. There were also salt-works, a Venetian discovery, which were able to support Venice with the salt needed, and export some to other countries. Of course, let us not forget that Crete, or at those times the Kingdom of Crete (Regno di Candia), as it was called, was under Venetian occupation up to 1210.

There was a six-year period (1204-1210) during with Crete was under Genoan occupation.

47

From left to right, the wall and the Carbonano angle, accompanied by the very tall Riva or Tiepolo bastion, which takes a auricular (curvilinear) shape. Its upper part is surrounded by a rocky, semicircular line (cordone), preserved in very good shape. The same architectural characteristics are also apparent in other parts of the fortification of the island.

Here, on the left hand side you may see the dock and today's entrance, as well as the ticket's office, just below the trees. On the right hand side there is the coffee shop, the public toilets and just below it, the rectilinear wall and the baronial Moceniga-Barbariga half-moon bastion.

ROVING ABOUT

This is today's entrance to the island, also called south gate. This is were the dome-shaped, 20-meters long tunnel lays, with eight arches, a really dark channel that led the lepers to the interior of the colony and into alienation, according to Hislop's novel.

The tunnel is built at the edge of the a uricular end (orecchione) of the Tiepolo or Riva bastion, invisible by the sea. In that way, it played an important role in the defence of the island, since it allowed the inhabitants to surprise the enemy.

At the old Venetian square, the guided tour has just started.

On the left hand side, you may see a beautiful Venetian mansion, with no roof but with a carefully preserved arch on the central living-room.

On the right hand side, walking upwards through the steps, there are two beautiful, renovated, two-floor houses, bearing mixed Turkish and Venetian characteristics. The Venetian character is apparent in the thick walls, the arches and arcs, the carved stones and the bars in the windows, the coloured doors and the wood-supported walls.

This Venetian-built road leads just behind the cannon holes of the rectilinear wall.

This Turkish fountain could be better preserved (bottom, left)

An old, home-oven, just next to the old, abandoned, two-roofed house, which attracts the eyes of the tourists and a second house, renovated, with an arresting front-wall.

The Carbonano arched gate, built in 1583. The details of the wall of the gate (on the left) and the latticed windows of the second floor (on the right) are surprising. The palm and eucalyptus tree, just in front of the empty houses give a pleasant feeling of freshness and life itself.

The market with Ottoman characteristics standing out, the two-floored buildings, the shops with their large doors, the coffee-shops and the latticed, glass windows have always been a place of attraction, a meeting point of the inhabitants of this island.

Detail. The grip of a door.

The lepers used to
spend the endless
hours of their isolation
playing cards,
backgammon and
other games, in an
effort to let go of the
distress.

A barely visible inscrip-
tion "ΚΑΦΦΕΝΕΙΟ"-
coffee-shop, just
above the arch of
Carbonano gate, is
a true reminder of
those times.

60

The renovation brought out the street and the shops. The flower pots with basil across the state museum are also a reminder of the Cretan villages. The local bakery is ready to be used and the interior of the houses long for the footsteps of the owners.

61

Uphill alley with steps, leading to the houses on the hill, above the market. Almost all vertical streets are quite similar. The renovation work paid its respects to the past, so everything remains the same. The entrances to houses, the gardens, the ovens, the fire-places, the drain pipes, the roofs are left untouched or respectfully renovated. Walking by those rugged alleys of the colony, a feeling of bitterness arises for those people who lived here and the unfair survival battle they had to fight. The lepers had to fight not only a physical war, but also a psychological and moral one. Besides the terrible, persistent pain of their broken limbs, they had to face social rejection, discrimination, lack of family warmth, as well as the everlasting stigma of the illness.

At this old, two-roofed renovated house, three signboards with the inscriptions "HOUSE OF KONDOMARI, PAPADIMITRIOU & KALLIOPI", take us back to the filming of the Greek TV series for MEGA channel, "The Island", based on the book "The Island" by Victoria Hislop.

Around Agios Pandeleimon church, a pebbled road begins, which leads upwards to the old leper hospital, the Turkish mosque and Agia Varvara church of the Venetians. There, the lepers would find medical care, comfort and solidarity. Further away, a nice stone staircase leads to the houses, on the side of the hill, just around the hospital (photos on the right-hand side).

The door and the windows of the hospital lay wide open. Some windows are protected by heavy, iron bars. What might be the reason for that? The corridor is empty, the rooms are empty and nobody is waiting for the doctor to visit. The basins, syringes, bottles, oil lamps and the rest of the medical apparatus left in this looted hospital, is exhibited at the island museum. Here lies total abandonment. View from the hospital window, during renovation works.

67

Around the hospital, the alley leads on top of the hill, towards the abandoned Agios Nikolaos church and the arched powder store room, underneath the thick shadow of the pine trees. A worn out by time fresco of Jesus Christ at the cupola of the temple is a reminder of the Byzantine period. Next to the temple you might see another rain water tank and its drain pipes, preserved in a fine state.

Agios Panteleimon church was built in 1709 by Iakovos Tziritas, as we notice on the inscription underneath the main entrance: "This temple of saint and great martyr Panteleimon was built on the 9th May, 1707, by Iakovos Tziritas, may God help his family". Later, in 1715, it was destroyed by the Turks, when they invaded the fortress and was rebuilt in 1900. In 1953, the lepers, having faith only in God and this saint, worked together and renovated this church.

And their prayers were indeed answered! The vaccine for leprosy was discovered in the United States (in fact, the cure for leprosy is not a vaccine but a medical treatment, which includes a group of chemotherapeutic drugs, mainly dapsone, which was discovered in 1948). This treatment was applied to the patients living in Spinalonga island and the illness started gradually to retreat. Leprosy could finally be cured and as time went by, was no longer considered a curse, as it was thought of in the past. As a result, the last cured lepers of Spinalonga island left to Athens in 1957.

Here you may see the Venetian basin and ponds, where women from all around Crete washed the lepers' clothes. The first basin was constructed in 1637. In the next photograph you may also see the chimneys of the ovens, used for the decontamination of the clothes.

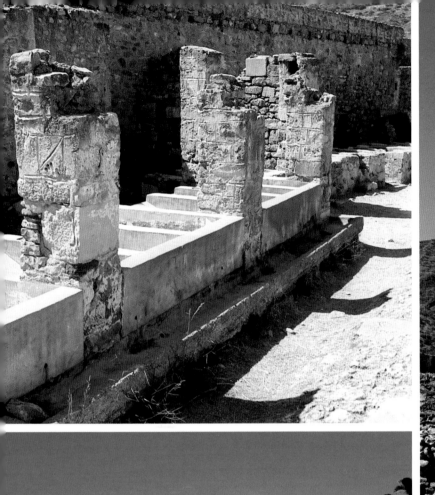

73

Depicted here are the main street and the small Turkish neighbourhood.

Two-roofed houses, with carved stone arches and entrances and a few pre-served wooden windows and doors.

Some houses are partly reconstructed, which help us imagine the past.

A sense of nobility is in the air.

The arched Venetian guard room, with the thick bars on the grand windows and the peculiar fire place, the latter decontamination room for the ill, parallel to the road leading to the main entrance of the castle and the old, Venetian port. On its interior, the old decontamination oven is finally protected. A few years back, it was left by the right hand side of the main gate to rot in the rain.

The small photo
on the left is borrowed
by the Spinalonga museum.

This small castle, situated on the point formed by the Fianco Genese angle, supervised and protected the main gate and the port at all times.

The pier of the old Venetian port. Here anchored all the battleships and merchant ships: Venetian galleys and galliots in the beginning and Turkish schooners and brigantines later on, transporting goods. Here, on the 13th October, 1904, Captain Fafoutis led the first lepers to the island and Captain Fourtounas used to anchor his boat, when bringing the post to the ill.

Here is the doubtlessly arresting central Venetian gate to the castle (Porta Maestra), Tuscany style, built in grey limestone, framed by two vertebrate semi-columns. At its top, half-destroyed, the same carved inscription seen at the Michiel bastion: "LUCAS MIC(HAEL), PRO(VVEDITOR) GE(NERALIS) R(EGNI) CR(ETAE)". Following the traditional benediction of the waters, Lucas Michael, the general intendant of Crete at those times, placed the founding stone on 15th June, 1579. The construction of the castle begun under the supervision of the architect-engineer Genese Bressani.

By the main street there are houses, some deserted and some partly renovated. Gates to the yards, roofs and floors that have fallen, cupboards and shelves on the walls, rudiments of Turkish bathrooms.

Water-pipe, which was probably used to supply a water-tank, underneath the pebbled mosaic.

"Walking on the streets of Spinalonga, stop and take a big breath. Coming from a house nearby, you may hear the grieving weep of a mother, a sister, or the sigh of a man. Let your tears flow... and you will see thousands of tears shining, tears which have fed this street".

Ep. Remoundakis

Window, overlooking the main street, the walls and the sea, up till the village of Plaka.

The priories were built in 1937, according to the graceless architectural style of the time.

84

The low, Michiel bastion, with its huge fenestras to fit the massive cannons. The passing-by ships had no chance of surviving! The boat just passing in front of the fenestra is in clear sight!

85

86

Some parts of the coastal waters were naturally inaccessible.

Here is the stairs, leading to the top of the hill, just besides traversa Molina, connection the wall of the sea to the wall of the top of the hill. Some of the steps are ruined.

This is Ragone point, strong and powerful. Those points defended the wall from attacks.

Later on, a few changes on the street beside the exterior wall took place, creating the impression that the wall is divided into two parts: the lower one by the sea and the upper, on the left hand side of the long, straight street.

This is the wide street leading to the double sanctorum church of Agios Georgios. This is where the last prayers for the dead lepers took place, who finally broke their bonds with life and were forever free of their unbearable anguish. On the wall by the entrance door to the church, an inscription with Byzantine letters says:

«Year 1661, 2nd of February. Remember, oh Lord, your son Ioannis Psalidis, master builder of Sitia and his wife Eleni and his father, Michael, and his mother Eleni and their children.»

On the north side of the church, a tree trunk is carved into a char, waiting in the shadow for the tired visitor.

91

Just in front of the church is the Bondumiero auricular point, with its characteristic watch tower and the water tanks behind it. On the left hand side, between the two streets you might see what is left from the old Muslim cemetery; on the far end, the open sea.

93

The square Donato bastion. Here, looking by the sea, sometimes peaceful and other wild, the lepers are rest in peace, underneath the stones. May God rest their souls! This place is definitely the perfect burial spot. Here, on this wind-protected, south-eastern edge of Spinalonga, where the sun is warm all year long, those ill people will no longer experience nightmare winters, freezing inside their crumble little houses.

In the past, some vandals took the shine off this sacred place, taking the lid off of those tombs.

This breathtaking bastion protected the eastern passage between Spinalonga and Kolokitha islands.
This sea passage was almost inaccessible.

Today, the boats pass with no fear, the watch-tower is empty.
The soldiers are no longer behind those deadly cannon fenestras! There is no sound of war, absolute peace reigns!

Just across Spinalonga, in Kolokitha island, one of the Venetian stone pits is clearly in view.

A recently built cement road, starting at the port and ending up the hill, leads though the fortification of the southern front wall and the fenestras of the southern wall (page on the right hand side).

This Venetian street, a cobblestone pavement with low steps, leads to the most impressive fortification work of all, Barbariga half-moon (mezzaluna), first-class built, with five huge arched cannon fenestras 4 meters wide, a work-out site and a sea-view site, surrounded by thirty five cannon fenestras. This was the pride of the Venetians and at the same time the dread of the enemy (see next pages).

At the front, low on the ground, between the second and third cannon fenestra, carved with skill on a stone, the winged lion of Saint Marcos dominates, a symbol of the Venetian democracy, walking towards the right and holding the Gospel open in its claws, a sign of time of peace and prosperity. A closer look allows us to read the following, moving words of Christ to his disciple: "PAX TIBI MARCE, EVANGELISTA MEUS", "May peace be with you, Marcos, my evangelist.

The Venetian Democracy wanted peace, though built castles and prepared the armies for war...
This is how things have always been...
Pax Romana...
Pax Veneziana...
Pax Americana...

On the left hand side, Mema and Faliera turrets or curtains (cortina) and Molino side (fianco) blocks the entrance to the city. Higher up, where the second turret with Barbariga half-moon meet, there is a small, roofed gate, which allows entrance to the famous Moceniga-Barbariga bastion (page on the left)

Those two entrances to the castle, which face each other, with their massive carved stones, are truly breath-taking.
In times of great need, the eastern entrance/exit allows permission to Donato bastion, within just a few steps. In that way, the Venetians invented a perfect hideout.

On the eastern entrance/exit, on the smooth and flat stones in the ground, on the most wind-protected south-eastern part of the island, the ill gathered, discussed, played games and looked at the sea. To make time go by easily, they used sharp objects –knives, nails or rocks- to carve simple sketches on the rocks (ships, sails, houses, abstract squares or even boards-games, like checkers, backgammon and chess).

This gate is called "gate of the mountain". The path leads to the top of the hill, to the Miani artillery square. Unfortunately, this square is today ruined. From this high up location the Venetian guards supervised the whole area and the sea passages.

The view is breath-taking.
A full rotation offers a panoramic, cinematographic view, which covers the whole island till the far shores of Kolokitha island and Crete, depicted in the next four photographs.

This triplet-arched building was definitely one of the Venetian soldiers' camps, the only one preserved in such a good state today.

The only arched building left standing today, just around the wall on the top of the hill. Apparently, it is one of the Venetian soldiers' camps. Next to it, a path travelling parallel to the wall, leading to the north-western side of the island.

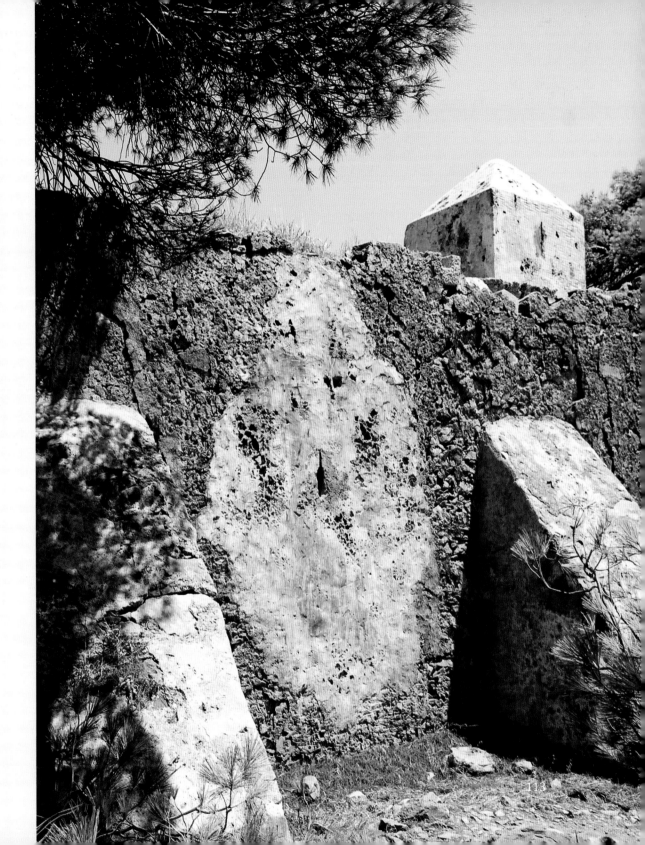

The top of the hill, surrounded by the internal fortification, is fully covered in pine trees.

On the steep north slope you may see Mostra and Moerta fortified sites, as well as Contarini point, with its gate, leading to the north, lower circumferential fortification belt.

Just across Spinalonga island, the village of plaka, mirroring in the waters.

The slope down to the colony is divided into small parts of land, which was cultivated at those times. However, their owners –Venetians, Turks and lepers- are now gone forever. Today, those lands are unattended to, nobody cares for them. The fig, prickly pear, almond and pine trees, the caper spices, wild horehounds, bitter cucumbers, the local plants, the daisies, pistachios are running wild. The wild plants have now covered even the old alleys. The fructiferous trees, that offered joy and treats to those hungry, have no longer a purpose and don't know what to do with their fruits.

Unfortunately, man remembers nature just occasionally.

117

The last cannon fire was delivered from Mocenico-Barbariga mezzaluna. The smoke seems to be still in the air, just above the bastion. And this is a sign of farewell.

On its right hand side, a pomegranate tree, a symbol of breeding, fertility and longevity sees us off. "See you again, Lady Spinalonga!"

Our small trek to Spinalonga, to the "island of the living-dead" of the past, ends somewhere here.

We visited two thousand years of history, we saw the walls, the bastions, the streets, rocks and buildings, tried to experience the efforts, the sacrifices, the expectations of each nation that lived on this island and traced the beauty of today.

May this coarse island, this formerly impenetrable fortress, this crowded Turkish settlement, this isolated leper sanatorium print a smile on our face and give us patience and hope for the future.

May this incomparable beauty, plunged in grief and tears, be further used for common good, to dress forever this idyllic spot of Merambellos.

About the "disease"

Leprosy, or otherwise Hansen' disease, is primarily an infectious disease, affecting the skin and skin nerves, causing skin lesions. In other words, the skin appears flaking, like fish scales. The Norwegian doctor Gerhard Hansen was the one who in 1873 discovered the mycobacterium causing leprosy (Mycobacterium leprae). While nerves undergo necrosis, the patient has no more the sense of cold, heat or pain and in return he/she is exposed to self-injuries that might cause severe infection.

The first symptom of leprosy is the appearance of big red and white spots on the skin, depending on the natural colour of the patient. Those skin areas undergo necrosis and can no longer transport information to the brain. At this stage, the illness can be cured, though it but must be treated immediately. At later stages of the illness, there is a general body disfigurement, mainly around the limps and face. Death occurs because of the infections caused by the illness to different vital organs of the body. Leprosy is considered a contagious disease, even though the type of contagion is not fully understood. It is thought that this disease spreads only when there is close and regular contact with someone carrying the bacteria. However, it is a fact that more than 95% of the general population is naturally immune to the leprosy mycobacterium.

This is a really old illness, dating to the depths of the Ages. It has first appeared in Egypt and India during 1500BC. As a disease, it was conveyed in Europe by the Roman troops. Leprosy was associated with curse and anathema, and this is why a leper has always been considered an outcast of society.

References

In Greek:

Αλιμπέρτης Αντώνης, *Ακολουθήστε μας στη Σπιναλόγκα,* Εκδόσεις Mystis, Ηράκλειο, 2006.

Αρκαδάκη Μαρία, *Το Φρούριο της Σπιναλόγκας 1571-1715,* Αγιος Νικόλαος, 2001.

Μακράκης Μανόλης, *Ελούντα – Η ιστορία της μέσα από την ιστορία της Κρήτης.* Ελούντα, 2009.

Μόσχοβη Γεωργία, *Σπιναλόγκα.* Αθήνα, 2009.

Παπαγεωργίου Κωστής, *Τα νησιά της Κρήτης.* Ηράκλειο, 1996.

Πεδιαδιτάκης Γεώργιος, *Ιστορία της Ελούντας.*

In English:

Beryl Darby, 1984, *Spinalonga: The Leper Island,* Efstathiadis Group.

Victoria Hislop, 2007, *The Island.* Harper Paperbacks.

By the same author, the tales:

Goodmorning, Lady Spinalonga

Hello, King Minos.

By the same Publisher:

Candia Veneziana